GW01372812

Original Title: Vikings Norse Mythology and Culture.

© Vikings Norse Mythology and Culture, Carlos Martínez Cerdá and Victor Martínez Cerdá, 2023

Authors: Victor Martínez Cerdá and Carlos Martínez Cerdá (V&C Brothers)

© Cover and illustrations: V&C Brothers

Layout and design: V&C Brothers

All rights reserved. This publication may not be fully or partially reproduced, stored, recorded or transmitted in any form or by any means, mechanical, photo-chemical, electronic, magnetic, electro-optical or by photocopying or information retrieval systems, or any other present or future means, without the prior written authorization of the "copyright" holders.

VIKINGS

NORSE MYTHOLOGY AND CULTURE

1

They never referred to themselves as Vikings.

It was not until the beginning of the 19th century that the word "Viking," of English origin, began to be used.

It was an adaptation of the word "vik," which meant inlet or bay, and it is also believed to have originated from the Old Norse word "vikingr," which meant pirate or raider.

There is still disagreement about its true origin and meaning.

The Vikings took some time to have a concept of nation for themselves.

The Viking Age began in 793, but it was not until 872 that Harald Fairhair became the first Scandinavian king, in his case of Norway.

Until then, they were led by local chieftains who controlled small territories.

The Franks called them "Normans," the Saxons called them "Danes," the Baltic peoples called them "Varangians," the Muslims called them "Urdumaniyyum," words that pointed to their Nordic origin, and the Byzantines called them "Rus" because of the reddish color of their hair.

2

They did not know how to spin wool to weave clothes.

Before learning to make their own woolen fabrics and importing them thanks to their incursions, the wool of sheep was of no use to them.

They only used them for their milk, meat, and skin.

We might think that a culture like that of the Vikings, who lived in cold climatic zones and sometimes extreme conditions, would be able to weave resistant and warm garments, but it was not the case.

Although they used the skins of domesticated or hunted animals to create leather for their clothes, they did not know how to spin wool fiber.

The Vikings' socks were created using a technique called "Nålebinding," which means "binding with a needle."

The method creates an elastic fabric that uses short wool threads and a single-eye needle that is often wide and flat.

The stitches are commonly but not always calibrated by wrapping them around the thumb.

It is a complicated technique with many points in common with crochet techniques.

It required a lot of experience and skill, but skilled hands were able to make socks very quickly.

3

The footwear was of terrible quality.

The Vikings' footwear was neither durable nor resistant despite living in a cold environment with harsh weather.

Snowy, wet, and icy conditions did not help them develop a good technique for creating waterproof and sturdy footwear.

The Vikings often lived with their feet constantly soaked.

The muddy terrain they lived in, the low side of their boats called "drakar," boats that constantly let in water due to the waves, and their livelihood of fishing on the coast all contributed to testing their footwear.

Their footwear was simple, poorly constructed, and barely lasted a month.

This has been demonstrated by the multitude of shoe dumps found in archaeological excavations throughout Scandinavia.

4

Why was the axe their preferred weapon?

Simply put, it was cheaper to make an axe than a sword.

Contrary to what is usually believed, soldiers in the European kingdoms of the time did not usually go equipped with a sword, which was considered a luxury item.

Their main weapon was the spear.

They used one or two-handed axes.

Scandinavia was full of trees, and every Viking warrior had worked wood to build their houses and boats with an axe from a very young age, which is where their skill and strength came from.

As lovers of close combat, the axe was a light, very effective weapon for breaking and tearing away shields by pulling them when stuck.

They were perfect for dismembering and cutting the necks of their enemies.

If you were equipped with chainmail, you could avoid being cut, but not a bone fracture after an axe blow, leaving their enemies completely exposed to a precise blow to the head or neck.

5

They were fascinated by exotic objects and figures.

The numerous journeys made by the Vikings took them
to the most remote places, establishing contacts
with many cultures of the time.

Figures, objects, and jewelry from other cultures and religions
excited them, not just Christian ones, anything that
seemed strange and eye-catching.

These objects were trophies that would help them recount
their stories and give greater credibility to their journeys and
incursions while getting drunk on mead around the fire
in their large Scandinavian cabins upon their return.

In 1954, a bronze figure of Buddha in the lotus position was
found during excavations on the island of Hëlgo,
believed to originate from Kashmir in India.

Other objects were found alongside this figure,
some of them religious, from Ireland and Egypt.

Textile archaeologist Annika Larsson from Uppsala University
in Sweden has studied fabrics from burial sites, finding Arabic
characters interwoven with golden thread on silk fabrics,
including the word "Allah."

It's not that some Vikings might have converted to Islam,
but for them, these characters were likely imbued with
some sort of mysticism.

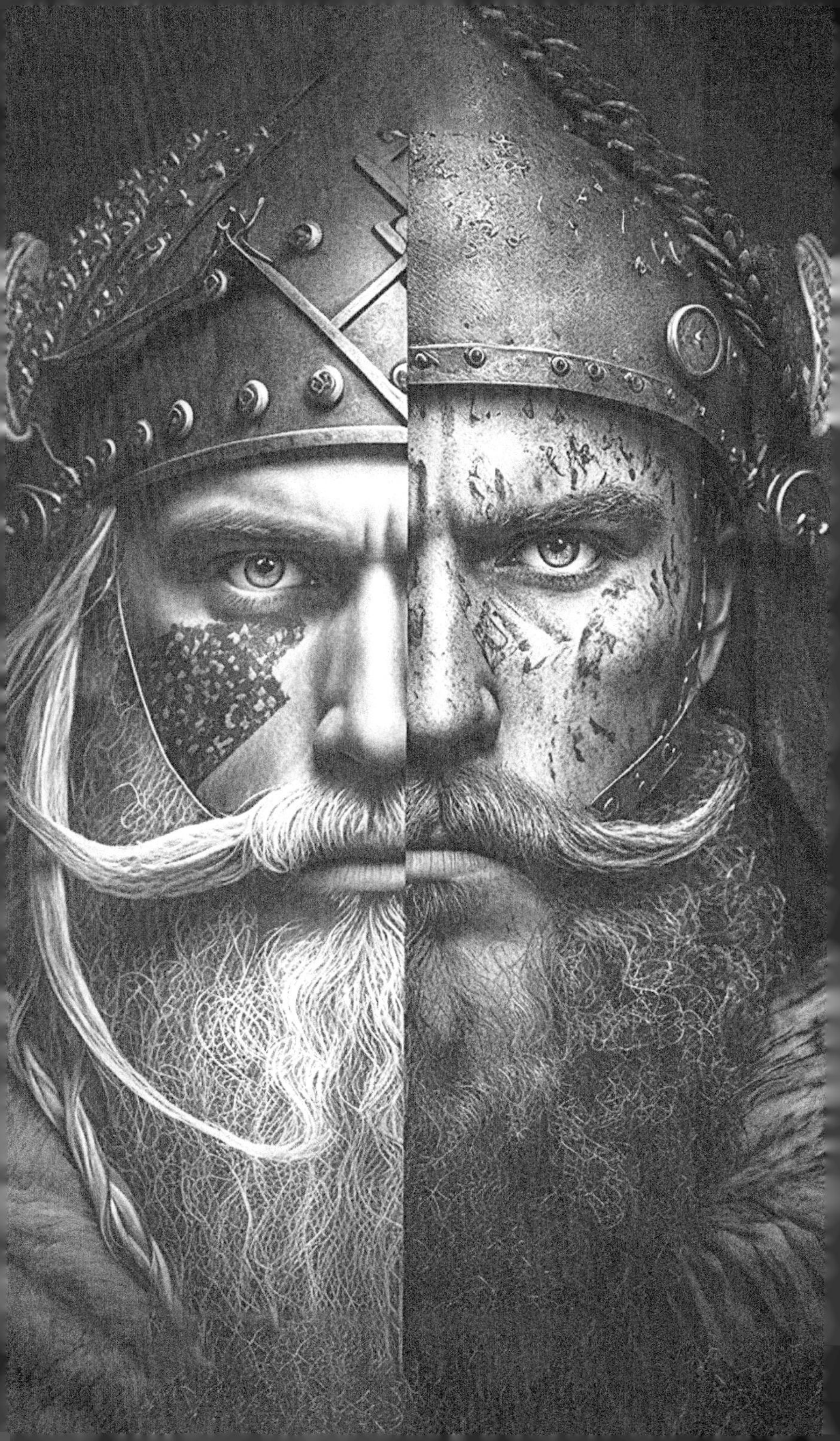

6

Creators of the "honeymoon" and lovers of mead.

The cold lands of Scandinavia didn't have fruit trees or vines to collect fruit for fermenting alcoholic beverages.

They only had honey with which to make mead, one of the oldest alcoholic beverages in human history.

It was heavily consumed by the Celts until the appearance of wine, which was much more productive.

But in these remote and inhospitable lands, it was the only thing that could be fermented.

The Vikings weren't beekeepers, but they managed to get bees to create their hives in places known to them.

Nevertheless, it was still difficult to obtain and find honey.

By fermenting water and honey, a beverage with between 5% and 15% alcohol content was obtained, depending on the amount of honey added.

It could be more or less sweet and even frothy.

Did you know that the term "honeymoon" has Viking origins?

Viking newlywed couples consumed mead every day during the first month after the wedding (28 days), believing that this ritual would help them conceive their first male child.

This custom was exported to the British Isles and Normandy, where the couples of the Saxon and Frankish population tried to secretly imitate this pagan tradition.

7

Vikings had a reputation for being dirty, savage people who smelled like sea and rotten, poorly tanned leather.

But what could be expected of men who disembarked from their drakkars on the beach after several days or weeks at sea, feeding on dried fish?

Ahmad ibn-Fadlan, an Arab writer and traveler from the 10th century, who was the inspiration for the movie "The 13th Warrior", came into contact with a squad of Swedish Vikings on the Volga River somewhere near the present-day city of Kazan in Russia.

He lived with them for several days and made a detailed description of them, but from the point of view of a refined member of the embassy of the Abbasid Caliphate of Baghdad.

"They are the filthiest creatures that God has created, they do not wash their hands after eating or having sex, not even after their bodily needs."

But the truth is that when they were not on raiding campaigns, they took great care of their hygiene and personal appearance.

They bathed frequently, both men and women, and frequently used their saunas.

They also took care of their beards and long hair.

They loved to perfume themselves and wear colorful clothes, display tattoos, and jewelry.

8

They made and consumed toxic bread.

Breadmaking was not their strong point; the lands where they lived were not ideal for growing wheat and rye.

Their diet was based on the consumption of fish, meat, dairy products, and vegetables.

The introduction of the plow that mixed the soil better than the primitive wooden plow in the late Viking era helped cultivate wheat and rye in a fruitful way.

Research has shown that the Vikings, due to their inexperience, misunderstood how to make flour and mixed in seeds of weeds like Bromus or Vallico, among many others, causing illness to those who consumed them.

9

They filed and colored their teeth.

In numerous excavations, burials and mass graves have been found, and upon analyzing human remains, it was discovered that many of the teeth were filed or sharpened.

The Vikings were very fond of trends and fashions, and it is possible that they underwent such a painful procedure to give themselves a more masculine appearance.

They also colored their teeth black, red, or any other color, using wax to which they added some type of natural dye to then apply it to their teeth.

As far as is known, filing and coloring of teeth was a widespread practice throughout Scandinavia during a certain period of time in the Viking era.

10

Harald Bluetooth and Bluetooth technology.

Danish king from 958 and also Norwegian from 970 until his death in 986.

He was known as Harald "Bluetooth" due to the blue color of one of his teeth, perhaps caused by fetal erythroblastosis.

The Swedish company Ericsson named its wireless data transmission technology, invented in 1994, Bluetooth (blue tooth) in honor of Harald Bluetooth.

The metaphorical name of the wireless technology that transmits data over short distances was based on the union that Harald Bluetooth created between the kingdoms of Denmark and Norway under the Christian religion, also adapting the symbol of his name found in some runic inscriptions.

The Bluetooth technology would connect all types and brands of devices that used it.

11

Helmets.

Most Vikings did not even use helmets, as demonstrated by the fact that only five Scandinavian helmets from the Viking era have been found.

Helmets were made of iron, a resource that they preferred to allocate to the manufacture of axes, knives, and swords.

In addition, during the era of raids, the Vikings rarely formed large cohesive armies that could make effective use of helmets.

The Vikings needed lightweight equipment, an axe, a knife, and maybe someone would carry a shield hanging on their back, they did not need more.

They would land, run, loot, and escape as quickly as possible with all the loot they could carry before any garrison realized their presence.

12

The raids.

The era of raids began at the start of the Viking Age, when the element of surprise was on their side.

Over the years, coastal populations began fortifying themselves, constructing watchtowers and deploying resources and soldiers to protect themselves.

From then on, the Vikings began colonizing through force, occupying much of the British Isles and coastal regions of the Baltic Sea.

This was the phase when they started collecting tributes from the local population.

Initially, they left small garrisons in the area, but they began demanding increasingly larger tributes and eventually formed kingdoms like York and regions under their control, such as the Danelaw in Britain.

Their wealth and garrisons grew, and they began to equip themselves properly with iron-capped armor and helmets.

The idyllic and savage image of the Vikings with their horned helmets comes from representations in Wagner's opera cycle in the mid to late 19th century, such as "The Ring of the Nibelung."

Horned helmets were impractical in combat and were only used by the elite to highlight their imposing presence.

13

Viking sorcerers would curse using a chant called "the galdr."

It was a hypnotic chant recited in falsetto (a technique of vibration of the vocal cords), practiced by sorcerers or magicians.

The galdr is a word from Old Norse that refers to an enchantment, but literally translates to "chant."

According to written evidence left by some Scandinavian historians from the Middle Ages, such as the Icelander Snorri Sturluson (1179-1241), the galdr was a chant with the intention of bewitching.

They were also used to cast spells, curses, attract storms, dull swords, and favor victories.

It was a complex technique, and only the most experienced sorcerers were capable of handling a power they considered dangerous.

14

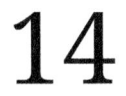

The first Tsar, Ivan "the Terrible", was a descendant of Vikings.

The Vikings who raided or provided their services to warlords on the banks of the Volga River in Russia were called "Varangians".

In the 9th century, a Varangian leader named Rurik traveled to the area as a mercenary to resolve territorial disputes between Slavic tribes.

When he did not receive the promised payment for his work, he settled down with his men and founded the city of Novgorod.

The long-lasting Rurik dynasty was created, and its descendants moved to Kiev, making it the capital of the so-called Kievan Rus, which later became Muscovy.

Ivan III "the Great" became the first ruler of unified Russia and ruled between 1462 and 1505.

One of the most well-known rulers was Ivan IV "the Terrible", the first to call himself tsar, who annexed new territories with extreme violence and ruled with great cruelty.

The Rurik dynasty lasted until 1598 with the death of the last ruler of this dynasty, Theodore I.

15

The Normans were descendants of Vikings.

The word Norman means "man of the north".

They were Vikings who settled at the mouth of the Seine River thanks to the "Treaty of Saint-Clair-sur-Epte" with the Frankish king Charles III "the Simple".

The Viking leader was named Hrolf Ganger, nicknamed "Rollo the Walker", and his mission was to protect the entrance of other Vikings through the mouth of the Seine that led to Paris.

"Rollo" himself participated in the siege of Paris in 885, as this and other important cities on the banks of the Seine had already been attacked on other occasions.

However, Charles III was determined that this should be the last one and made a drastic decision, taking the risk of putting the wolf to guard the hens.

Around the year 911, he appointed "Rollo" as Duke of Normandy and entrusted him with a mission that he fulfilled with flying colors, but at a high cost to the future of the kingdom of France.

The descendants of "Rollo" expanded their territory, taking it from France and creating an independent Duchy of Normandy that waged several wars with France.

The descendants of the Viking dynasty of the House of Normandy reached their peak in 1066 when William I "the Conqueror" claimed the throne of England, invaded it, and became king.

His descendants perpetuated even further, ruling England until 1135.

16

They visited America 500 years before Columbus.

The Saga of Erik the Red and The Saga of the Greenlanders tell the story of the Viking explorer Leif Eriksson (970-1020), the second son of another great explorer named Erik the Red, who founded the first Viking settlement in Greenland.

Leif Eriksson set out to reach some lands that he had heard about from the accounts of another explorer named Bjarni Herjólfsson.

Bjarni Herjólfsson recounted that his expedition became lost while trying to return to Greenland and the winds pushed them westward where they spotted a flat, green, wooded land.

But he refused to set foot on land because the winds became favorable again towards the east and he did not want to waste any more time or supplies.

They assumed that these were new lands to discover because they lacked glaciers and snow, and it was a warm land.

It is believed that he sighted the coasts of the Labrador Peninsula in Canada.

This story was recorded in the sagas mentioned above.

In around the year 1000, Leif Eriksson, fascinated by this story, set out westward to discover these lands.

That same year, he arrived at the island of Newfoundland where he created a small colony.

Leif described this land as green, rich in salmon, pastures, and vines, which he called Vinland (land of wines).

The Vikings used to give attractive names to the lands they discovered to attract new settlers. For example, Greenland means "green land".

Norwegian archaeologists Anne Stine and Helge Ingstad discovered the remains of a Viking settlement at L'Anse aux Meadows in the north of Newfoundland.

Investigations indicate that the Vikings never established themselves in America, but they probably visited it frequently from Greenland to gather wood.

17

Their descendants reigned in Sicily.

Roger I of Altavilla and Hauteville was a Norman nobleman nicknamed "the Great Count," son of the Norman nobleman Tancred of Hauteville.

He established himself in southern Italy as a vassal of his brother Robert Guiscard and participated in the reconquest of the island, which was then under Muslim rule.

His son Roger II became the first king of Sicily after the death of his brother Simon, and the Hauteville dynasty would reign in Sicily until 1198.

The interference of the Pope forced a change in the dynastic succession, which passed into the hands of the Hohenstaufen dynasty and later became part of the Holy Roman Empire.

Under Norman rule, Sicily became a melting pot of cultures, with Arabs, Normans, and Byzantines living together in peace.

Additionally, the island became prosperous thanks to the agricultural techniques established by the Arabs.

It was a court that loved culture, as exemplified by the famous geographical work called "The Book of Roger" or "Kitab Ruyar," the result of the travels made by the Andalusian traveler and explorer Al-Idrisi, financed by King Roger II.

18

They were great fans of competitive sports.

The enthusiasm of the Vikings for sports competition was probably not much different from ours.

They always tried to find out who was the strongest or most skilled in certain disciplines, such as hand-to-hand combat, sword fighting, spear throwing, running, and even jumping between the oars of a boat as if it were an obstacle course.

They also enjoyed horse fights, mountain climbing, knife juggling, swimming races, skiing, and, above all these disciplines, they loved a violent variant of hockey or football with a ball called Knattleik.

The rules of this sport are not clear, but in numerous Viking sagas, it is mentioned as apparently brutal.

For them, it was valid to reach Valhalla if you died practicing it.

It is known that it involved hitting a hard ball apparently made of tar with a stick, there was strong physical contact, and the use of hands was allowed, but it is not clear whether the goal was to score points or disqualify participants.

Verbal intimidation, shouting, and physical aggression were allowed.

According to the sagas, competitions were held between teams that could last all day, and there was a huge audience.

Apparently, it was quite an event.

This sport is still being recreated in Scandinavian countries and Canada today.

19

They were close to creating an empire.

King Canute II of Denmark and first of England came close to becoming the Viking emperor of an empire that some historians have referred to as the "North Sea Empire".

He inherited, conquered, or ruled Denmark, Norway, England, and territories in southern Sweden.

But succession disputes and the church prevented this empire from being created.

He married Aelfgifu Aelfhelmsdotter, the daughter of a Danish knight according to Norman tradition, something frowned upon by the church, which did not recognize her as a wife, so he remarried Emma of Normandy, a devout Christian widow of a deceased rival of the King of England, Ethelred II "the Unready," from whom he inherited the throne after his death thanks to a treaty they both had.

On his deathbed, King Canute tried to please all his male children by dividing the kingdom between Canute Hardeknut, Emma's son who inherited Denmark, the sons of Aelfgifu would inherit the rest, for Sweyn it would be Norway and for Harold England, who died in 1040, leaving the throne in the hands of his stepbrother Canute III Hardenkund who died soon after, in 1042, leaving the throne once again in Anglo-Saxon hands.

20

The legend of the last berserker.

They were mythologized for their extreme fierceness in combat.

Devout warriors who were followers of Odin, devoted to their gods in search of Valhalla to impress them and secure the best seats in the "hall of the fallen," they fought semi-naked or covered in bear or wolf skins.

Before battles, they tried to reach a trance state by consuming hallucinogenic mushrooms, foaming at the mouth and screaming like wild animals, sowing terror among their enemies, but also among the Vikings, as in that state, it was difficult for them to distinguish who was friend or foe.

They did not usually act cohesively with the rest of the Vikings in formations, they usually launched themselves alone against the enemy or were reserved for the moment when the battle began to be lost.

This was the case of the one known as the "last berserker."

No one ever knew his name or who he was, but his story was told by his own Saxon enemies whom he faced.

In the battle that led to the end of the "Viking Age," the "Battle of Stamford Bridge," Harald Hardrada's troops, also known as the "last Viking," crossed the bridge over the Derwent River to regroup and attempt a counterattack.

They needed to buy time, so they put a berserker in charge of guarding and slowing down the advance of the Saxon troops pursuing Harald Hadrada.

According to the Anglo-Saxon Chronicle, an enormous berserker over 2 meters tall, bare-chested, and armed with a huge axe defended the bridge, holding back the Saxon troops for an hour.

It is said that he killed 40 soldiers before being pierced by spears from soldiers who submerged themselves in the river and killed him from under the bridge.

21

They gave Latin languages and English many words.

Their nautical technology, whose contribution was enormous, and customs gave rise to words that were adopted by all cultures and became part of their dictionaries.

Well-known nautical words such as "abordar" (to board), "babor" (port), "barloa" (sternpost), "carlinga" (gunwale), "estribor" (starboard), "flota" (fleet), "guindaste" (derrick), "quilla" (keel), among many others.

Their customs also left us words such as "club," "esquí" (ski), "equipar" (to equip), "guindar" (to hang), "tinglado" (shack), "saga," "runa."

They also gave names to geographical features or unknown animals for everyone at that time such as "fiordo" (fjord), "géiser" (geyser), or "reno" (reindeer).

22

Course error.

The "Luna Raid" occurred in 860 AD during the Viking invasions of Europe.

The story goes that a group of Vikings, led by a warrior named Björn Ironside, decided to launch a raid into the Mediterranean with the goal of plundering rich and prosperous cities.

The Vikings' original intention was to attack the city of Rome, but due to a lack of geographic knowledge and adverse weather conditions, they ended up veering off course and arriving at the city of Luna, which is located in the Tuscany region of Italy.

There, the Vikings were surprised by the wealth and luxury of the city, which was full of treasures and valuable artifacts.

The Vikings plundered and destroyed Luna, causing a great deal of damage and killing many of the city's inhabitants.

However, after their attack, they realized that they had not attacked Rome as they had originally planned.

The confusion was probably due to the fact that Italian cities at that time shared many architectural and cultural characteristics, making them difficult to identify.

This incident illustrates the unpredictable nature of Viking invasions and how the Vikings could change their target at any moment.

Additionally, it also shows the Vikings' ability to adapt to different conditions and situations, even when they were not familiar with the terrain and geography of the area.

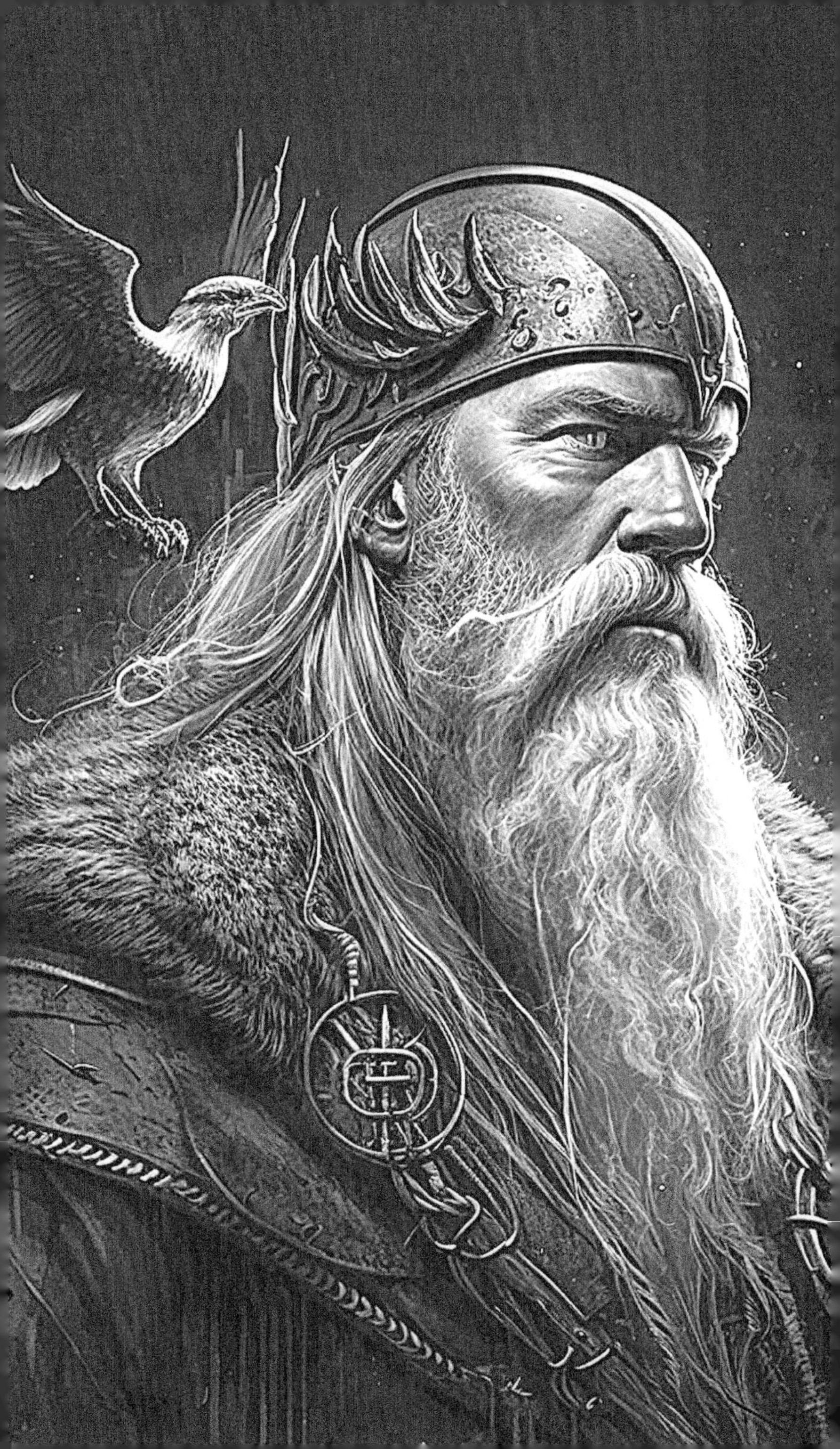

23

Religion and beliefs.

They had a multitude of gods, divided into the Æsir and Vanir clans, and multiple mythological stories that they always kept in mind both in their battles and in the time they spent taking care of and maintaining their villages.

Among their beliefs, for example, it is known that they thought that if they died in battle, they would be chosen to join Odin in the halls of Valhalla while they waited and prepared for the arrival of Ragnarok.

On another note, it is also known that they had beliefs about the origin of the world, which is explained in the legend of Midgard.

In this, it is told that in the beginning of time, everything was jungle and desert and that the Norse gods, as pioneers, cleared it, creating space for both themselves and humans to live.

24

The role of Viking women.

Conceiving a girl was not a pleasant experience for the Vikings.

Many times, if a couple's first child was a girl, she was left in the forest to die so that the mother would not have to raise her, which would accelerate a new pregnancy that was expected to result in a boy.

The life expectancy of women was approximately 35 years due to childbirth complications.

They played a fundamental role in settlements and in the creation of new societies.

Furthermore, contrary to what one might think, the rights of Nordic women, when they got married, were better in Viking society than in other places in Europe or in later periods.

They were the owners of the keys to the main house and when their husbands were not around, they were in charge of both the slaves and the estate.

We even know that they had the right to divorce for various reasons and, like men, could inherit and own property.

25

In Viking culture, they believed in the existence of magic and the possibility that wounds could be caused by some type of spell.

That is why Viking doctors not only focused on healing physical wounds, but also on eliminating any magical influence that could be affecting the patient.

Regarding the use of onions and leeks, these were considered medicinal plants and were used in the preparation of various remedies to treat various ailments, including wounds.

In addition, it was believed that these plants had disinfectant properties and helped reduce inflammation.

As for licking blood from a wound, although it may sound strange to us today, it was a common practice for the Vikings.

They believed that by tasting the blood, they could identify the type of wound and, therefore, determine what type of treatment should be applied.

In addition, it was believed that the doctor's saliva had healing properties that could aid in the wound's healing process.

26

According to Norse mythology, the first man and woman were created from the sweat of the armpit of a giant named Ymir.

The man was named Ask and the woman was named Embla.

In addition, the Vikings believed that the sky was held up by four dwarves named North, South, East, and West.

Norse religion also included the belief in a series of gods, including Odin, Thor, and Freya, among others.

The Vikings believed that the gods controlled many aspects of life, including war, fertility, and weather.

As for the afterlife, the Vikings believed that warriors who died in battle were taken to Valhalla, a hall in the realm of the gods reserved for fallen warriors.

There, they were offered a life of battle and eternal glory.

Those who died of natural causes or diseases were not considered worthy of entering Valhalla and instead went to another realm called Hel, which was not a place of fire like in Christianity, but a frozen place.

27

The murder of Edmund II of England by a Viking in the year 1016 is a historical event known as the "Death of Edmund."

The Viking who committed the murder was called Thorkell the Tall according to some sources, but the identity of the killer remains uncertain.

According to the Anglo-Saxon Chronicle, Edmund II, also known as Edmund the Martyr, had been captured by the Danes and was tortured and killed for refusing to renounce his Christian faith.

However, in the 12th century chronicle of Roger of Hoveden, the story of the king's murder by a Viking in the royal latrine is told.

According to this version, the assassin infiltrated the king's fortress and hid in the latrine.

When the king sat down to do his business, the Viking stabbed him with a dagger in the backside.

The resulting wound was fatal and Edmund died shortly thereafter.

This story is considered by some historians to be a legend or exaggeration, as Roger of Hoveden's chronicle was written several centuries after the events.

However, there may be some truth to the story, as Vikings often used infiltration and surprise tactics in their attacks.

In any case, the death of Edmund II was a significant event in England's history and had important political implications in the struggle for the throne between the Danes and the Anglo-Saxons.

28

Many words in the English language originate from Old Norse or Viking language, which was spoken by the Scandinavians during the time of Viking invasions in England and other countries.

Some of the words derived from Old Norse include:

- Anger: from Old Norse "ira", meaning anger or wrath.

- Kidnapping: from Old Norse "seka", meaning to take as a hostage.

- Plagiarize: from Old Norse "plaga", meaning to harm or hurt.

- To shout: from Old Norse "gráta", meaning to cry or whine.

- Hit: from Old Norse "golp", meaning blow or shock.

- Massacre: from Old Norse "meyslaht", meaning killing of kinsmen.

- Fleas: from Old Norse "fleas", meaning fleas.

- Dirty: from Old Norse "skyr", meaning dirty or impure.

- Ruthless: from Old Norse "hardr", meaning hard or merciless.

- Fear: from Old Norse "marr", meaning fear or dread.

- Rage: from Old Norse "fyrr", meaning fury or anger.

- To go mad: from Old Norse "liga", meaning to go crazy.

- Rotten: from Old Norse "rotna", meaning to rot.

- Mistake: from Old Norse "vísbending", meaning wrong indication or advice.

Other words derived from Old Norse are softer in meaning, such as "welcome" from Old Norse "velkominn", meaning received with joy, "gentle" from Old Norse "ginnheilagr", meaning holy or divine, and "tart" from Old Norse "tortta", meaning cake.

29

The children's song "London Bridge is Falling Down" has its roots in a Viking attack on London.

According to legend, in the 11th century, Vikings attacked the city and destroyed London Bridge, which was the only bridge crossing the River Thames at that time.

In the song, the lyrics describe how the bridge is falling down and how the queen, soldiers, and horses are falling into the water.

Although the song has Viking origins, it has evolved over the centuries and become a popular children's song.

The modern version usually has a longer lyric and a different melody than the original.

However, the song still retains the reference to London Bridge and its fall at the hands of the Vikings.

Lyrics of the modern version of the children's song:

London Bridge is falling down, falling down, falling down.

London Bridge is falling down, my fair lady.

Build it up with wood and clay, wood and clay, wood and clay.

Build it up with wood and clay, my fair lady.

The bridge is down with a big boom, big boom, big boom.

The bridge is down with a big boom, my fair lady.

Under the water, queen is found, queen is found, queen is found.

Under the water, queen is found, my fair lady.

Soldiers couldn't save her, save her, save her.

Soldiers couldn't save her, my fair lady.

London Bridge has fallen down, fallen down, fallen down.

London Bridge has fallen down, my fair lady.

30

They liked to make word games, although they didn't always rhyme.

Poem about a battle of Erik the Viking:

Red flames swallowed men and roofs.

As we grew furious, we cut off their breasts.

Scarred bodies lay sleeping.

Spread out in the streets.

The Vikings enjoyed playing with words, using alliteration and metaphor, and creating clever word games.

The poem we mentioned is a description of a battle of Erik the Viking, and shows some of these poetic features.

The use of alliteration in the first line, "Red flames swallowed men and roofs," helps to create a vivid and evocative image of the destruction that occurs during the battle.

The second line, "As we grew furious, we cut off their breasts," shows the use of metaphor to describe the violence of the battle.

In this case, the Vikings are not only cutting their enemies, but are "cutting" their strength and bravery.

The third line, "Scarred bodies lay sleeping," shows another metaphor to describe the lifeless bodies that remain after the battle.

The use of the word "scarred" suggests that the bodies are marked as if they were plowed fields, and the description of the bodies as "sleeping" is another metaphor to describe death.

31

When they invaded England, the Vikings liked to attack easy targets.

That's why they first targeted monasteries, like the one in Lindisfarne.

This event is considered the beginning of the Viking Age in England.

In the year 793, a group of Vikings from Denmark and Norway attacked the monastery of Lindisfarne, located on the northeast coast of England.

This monastery was an important center of learning and religion, and its plundering was an unprecedented act.

The Vikings chose to attack the monastery because it was an easy target and rich in loot, as the monks possessed valuable objects such as relics and illuminated manuscripts.

In addition, the monks were unarmed and not expecting an attack, so they were unable to defend themselves.

From this event, the Vikings began to make regular raids on the coasts of England, attacking and plundering other monasteries and coastal towns.

As they spread through the territory, the Vikings founded settlements and established their presence in the region.

32

Many Vikings did not know how to read or write, as most of them did not have access to formal education.

However, some Vikings could read and write in their native language, Old Norse, and runic inscriptions have been found on objects and monuments that were created by Vikings.

As for the information we have about the Vikings, much of it comes from sources written by Christian monks who were kidnapped by the Vikings during their raids in Europe.

These monks wrote chronicles and detailed accounts of their experiences with the Vikings, which gives us a valuable insight into their culture and way of life.

Additionally, there are also other sources of information about the Vikings, such as archaeological objects that have been found in tombs, settlements, and other places of interest.

These objects include weapons, jewelry, tools, and other artifacts that give us an idea of the skills and interests of the Vikings.

33

During the medieval period, hunting swans and consuming their meat was an exclusive activity of the nobility and royalty in England.

This was because swans were considered noble birds, and their meat was considered an exquisite delicacy.

In the 15th century, King Henry VII passed a law known as the "Swan Hunting Act," which stated that only members of the royalty and their guests could hunt and eat swans.

This law was in effect for several centuries, and although it is no longer applicable today, swans are still considered property of the Crown.

In fact, the "Swan Upping" is an annual ceremony that takes place in Britain, in which wild swans are captured, marked, and released back into the wild.

This ceremony is a way of verifying the ownership of swans, and it has been carried out since medieval times.

As for the Viking law, there is no written law that grants the people ownership rights over swans in Hornington, but there is a local tradition that establishes this belief.

In any case, it is important to note that the ownership of swans in England is protected by law, and anyone who captures or kills a swan without authorization may face criminal charges.

34

Vikings living in medieval Iceland built their houses inside turf mounds, an architectural technique known as "turf building".

These mounds were constructed from the soil and grass extracted from the ground, forming a solid and sturdy structure.

As for the windows, many of these houses did not have them, or only had a small opening at the top to allow light in.

This was partly due to Iceland's extreme weather conditions, with strong winds and very low temperatures, making it difficult to keep windows closed and protect oneself from the cold.

As for the use of cow dung as fuel for making fire, it is possible that some Vikings used it, although it was not a widespread practice.

Vikings used different types of fuel, such as wood, turf, and animal manure, to make fire and heat their homes.

The smoke and smell inside these houses were a problem, but it also helped keep insects and other unwanted animals at bay.

Overall, Viking houses in Iceland were dark and small, but they were also efficient in terms of heat conservation and protection against extreme weather.

In addition, Vikings also built other structures, such as farms and community buildings, that were larger and allowed for greater social interaction.

35

The Viking axe was one of the most popular and distinctive weapons used by Vikings in the Middle Ages.

These axes were practical and functional tools, but also considered symbols of status and prestige in Viking culture.

It is true that, in many cases, Viking axes were passed down from parents to children for generations as a way of maintaining and preserving family tradition.

In addition, these weapons were believed to have sentimental and emotional value, and often attributed with magical and protective qualities.

It is also worth noting that some Viking blacksmiths would inscribe runes on the weapons, including axes, to increase their power and protection.

Runes were a writing system used by Vikings to communicate and convey messages, but were also believed to have spiritual and magical properties.

Furthermore, some Viking blacksmiths would also decorate axes with intricate designs and motifs, which often had symbolic or spiritual significance.

These designs included geometric patterns, animal figures, and mythological motifs such as dragons and serpents.

Overall, Viking axes were highly valued tools and weapons in Viking culture and were considered an important element of Viking identity and tradition.

36

Vikings greatly valued oral storytelling and had a specific space dedicated to sharing and listening to stories, known as the "house of tales" or "hall of listeners".

There, people would gather to share stories and legends, often accompanied by music and songs performed by troubadours and musicians.

These oral stories were very important to Viking culture, as they transmitted stories of their ancestors, heroes, and deities, and also served to teach values and moral lessons through the adventures and challenges of the story's characters.

The Icelandic sagas are a famous example of the stories Vikings would tell.

These sagas are extensive prose narratives that detail the lives and exploits of Viking ancestors, and also include stories about gods and mythological creatures.

Many of the Nordic myths and legends we know today originated from these sagas and other Viking oral tales.

Vikings also valued poetry and music, and often used these mediums to express their emotions and tell stories.

Skalds were poets and bards who specialized in the creation and recitation of epic poetry, and often were part of Viking royal courts.

37

The Vikings were very superstitious and firmly believed in the existence of gods and spirits.

Viking religion was polytheistic, meaning they worshiped various gods and goddesses, such as Odin, Thor, Freyja, and Loki, among others.

The Vikings believed that gods and spirits influenced their daily life and luck in war and navigation, so they made offerings and rituals to honor them and ask for their protection.

They also believed that spirits inhabited nature, such as rivers, forests, and mountains, and that they should be respected and honored.

The figures they carried on the prow of their Viking ships were known as "figureheads" or "dragon heads," and often represented mythological creatures such as snakes, dragons, or gods.

The Vikings believed that these figures had protective powers and could scare the spirits and gods of the lands they attacked, giving them an advantage in war.

When the Vikings arrived at their own shores, they removed the figureheads from their ships so as not to offend their own protective gods and spirits.

The Vikings also believed in magic and witchcraft and used amulets and talismans to protect themselves from evil spirits and curses.

38

Viking society was divided into different social classes:

-The jarls were the local leaders, the nobles or kings, and were the only ones who could own land and exercise justice.

-The karls, on the other hand, were the working class of Viking society, made up of warriors, artisans, blacksmiths, ship builders, and other manual laborers. The karls were free and could own their own land and property.

-The thralls, on the other hand, were slaves and their social position was the lowest in Viking society. They were captured in wars or bought in slave markets and their functions were mainly agricultural and construction, although they could also perform tasks related to service and any other labor assigned to them, as they had no right to refuse. In addition, they were not allowed to carry weapons. The thralls were the property of their masters and could be bought, sold, gifted, or freed. Although not all Vikings owned slaves, the richest ones usually had several in their homes.

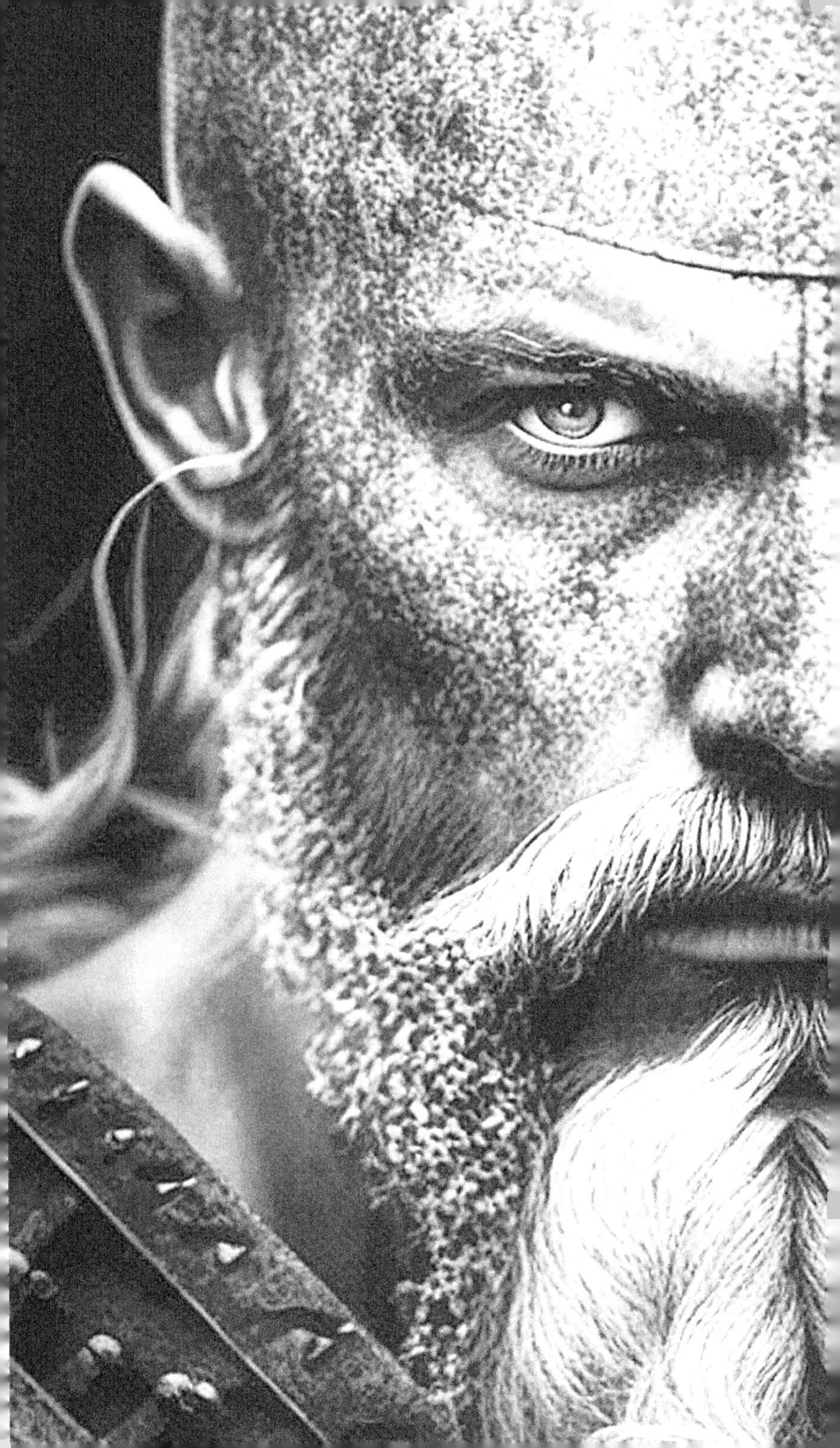

39

In Viking society, children were considered adults from the age of 12 and were assigned important responsibilities such as caring for animals or helping with household chores.

In addition, children were educated at home by their parents and learned practical skills such as hunting, fishing, navigation, and craftsmanship.

Formal education was provided in schools located in urban centers and was reserved for the children of the nobles and privileged classes.

There, young people learned to read, write, and perform basic calculations.

They were also taught poetry, history, and religion.

In Viking society, social ascent was possible through personal merit and achievements.

Therefore, even children born into low-class families or as slaves could rise to positions of power and accumulate great wealth over their lifetimes, if they demonstrated outstanding skills and achievements.

40

Vikings did not have buttons, so they used different types of brooches to fasten their garments.

The brooches could be simple or highly elaborate, and were a way to demonstrate the social status of the wearer, as the most ornate brooches were reserved for the nobles.

In addition to brooches, they also used cords and straps to adjust their clothing.

Regarding film adaptations, it is common for certain creative liberties to be taken to make the story more visually appealing.

Although these adaptations may not be entirely historically accurate, they can help to generate interest in a particular time period.

41

Vikings used skis to travel over snow and ice.

In fact, skis were a very useful mode of transportation in the Nordic countries, where cold and snowy weather was common for much of the year.

The skis used by the Vikings were simple and resembled modern cross-country skis more than the alpine skis used today.

Viking skis were made of wood and were approximately 2 meters long.

The Vikings used them for transportation, as well as for hunting and warfare.

In addition, it is believed that the Vikings were among the first to use skis in competitive sports.

42

Viking houses were known as "longhouses" and were usually built with wood and stone, with timber-framed walls and gable roofs covered in thatch or turf.

The turf provided good thermal and acoustic insulation, as well as protection against moisture.

Longhouses were spacious and divided into different sections for different purposes, such as food and tool storage, kitchen, dining area, and sleeping quarters.

In Iceland, some of these turf-roofed houses have survived to this day, such as in the case of Keldur, a village that has several of these types of houses.

These houses usually have a wooden structure covered with earth and turf, giving them a camouflaged appearance that blends in perfectly with the landscape.

43

Vikings typically had a diet based on animal products since they were excellent hunters and fishermen.

The most common foods in their diet were fish, meat (primarily pork and beef), milk, cheese, and butter.

They also consumed grains, mainly barley and rye, and legumes such as peas and lentils.

In addition to honey, they also used herbs and spices to season their meals.

Salt was an important ingredient in their diet, and they obtained it through the evaporation of seawater.

Vikings were also experts in making alcoholic beverages, such as beer and mead (a fermented drink made from honey).

Alcohol consumption was very common in Viking society and was considered an important part of social and religious life.

It is worth noting that, although Vikings are often portrayed as barbaric and violent, they also cared about hygiene and personal cleanliness.

For example, they used to bathe weekly and used combs and razors for personal grooming.

44

The search for wealth was one of the main motivations that drove the Vikings to raid other lands, but the reason behind the Viking Age is much more complex.

During the 8th and 9th centuries, Scandinavian countries like Norway, Sweden, and Denmark faced a series of political, economic, and social challenges, which led to territorial expansion and greater population mobility.

The Vikings were largely farmers and fishermen, but as the population increased and the demand for goods and resources grew, many were forced to seek other forms of subsistence.

Additionally, high taxes and oppression from ruling elites were also factors that led some to seek opportunities elsewhere.

Another important factor in the Viking Age was the development of new naval technologies, which allowed the Vikings to explore and colonize new lands.

Viking ships were fast and maneuverable, allowing them to navigate shallow waters and cross rivers to reach coastal towns and cities.

In summary, the Viking Age cannot be attributed to a single cause, but was the result of a complex series of political, economic, and social factors that led the Vikings to explore, trade, and conquer new lands.

45

The Vikings were well aware of their reputation and would kill women and children mercilessly as a way to maintain it, instilling fear among the settlements so that when they arrived, there would be no resistance.

However, the Vikings did not kill women and children mercilessly as a general practice.

In fact, while Norse sagas and other historical sources speak of the violence and cruelty of the Vikings in some instances, there are also many accounts of Vikings who respected women and children and even cared for their well-being during their raids.

Additionally, while the Vikings did attack settlements and cities, in many cases they did so with the intention of obtaining loot and riches, not necessarily to kill all the inhabitants.

It is important not to fall into stereotypes and to understand that the Vikings were a complex and diverse society with their own norms and values.

46

The Vikings used sundials to navigate during their sea voyages.

These sundials consisted of a vertical object (such as a pole or a rod) that cast a shadow on a horizontal surface (such as a plate or a board), and relied on the position of the sun to measure time.

The Vikings could also measure the position of the sun in the sky using the shadow of a pole stuck in the ground, and adjusting the pole until the shadow had a specific length.

In addition to sundials, the Vikings also used stars to navigate during the night. They knew the location of certain stars and constellations, and could use them to navigate at sea.

In particular, they used the North Star (Polaris) to find the North, and the constellation of the Big Dipper to find the North and the South.

As for the "magic crystals," it is believed to refer to the "sunstone" in English.

This stone was a transparent mineral such as calcite or cordierite, which the Vikings used to determine the position of the sun even on cloudy or snowy days.

By looking through the stone in the direction of the sun, the Vikings could detect the polarization of light and determine the location of the sun in the sky.

However, the historical evidence on the use of sunstones by the Vikings is limited and controversial.

47

The Vikings were known for their warrior skills and conquests, but they were also successful traders who established trade routes that spanned from Scandinavia to the Middle East and North Africa.

In Viking times, trade was a very important activity for the economy of Nordic societies.

The Vikings exchanged goods with other regions and cultures, and this allowed them to obtain resources that were not available in their own territory.

The Vikings traded products such as furs, wool, iron, wood, and agricultural products.

The Viking expansion allowed the establishment of new trade routes, and the Vikings became intermediaries between the Muslim and Christian worlds.

They established trade relations with the Byzantine Empire and the Abbasid Caliphate in the 9th century, importing spices, jewelry, silks, and other luxury goods.

They also traded with the Slavic peoples of Eastern Europe, and commercial exchanges were mainly conducted in markets in important cities such as Hedeby in Denmark, Birka in Sweden, and Kaupang in Norway.

48

The Vikings had different types of ships that adapted to their needs.

One of the most famous was the longship, a fast and maneuverable warship that had a raised bow and stern decorated with animal motifs, which gave them their name of "dragon".

These ships were long and narrow, and could carry up to 60 men, allowing them to move quickly and attack effectively.

On the other hand, knarrs were larger and more robust ships used for transporting goods.

They were less maneuverable than longships, but could carry large amounts of cargo and livestock.

The Vikings also used another type of ship, the snekkjas, which were smaller and faster than knarrs, and were mainly used for coastal raids.

Viking ships were built with oak, pine, or birch wood, and their design was very advanced for their time.

The hull was made up of overlapping planks, nailed and sewn together, giving them great strength and flexibility.

In addition, the Vikings used square sails and oars, allowing them to navigate with great precision both in open sea and coastal waters.

49

Viking Runes.

The Vikings had their own alphabet based on the Germanic runic script known as "futhark".

These Scandinavian Viking peoples engraved important events on stones, which are known as runestones.

In general, runestones record the heroic deeds of a particular leader and his men, or speak of successful campaigns abroad.

Much of what is known today about the Vikings comes from these inscriptions on stones found in Scandinavia, the British Isles, or even the Black Sea.

Viking runes had angular shapes to facilitate carving both on stone and wood.

The Vikings believed that writing was a "power" that humans possessed, and it was Odin himself who gave the runes to humans, taking them from the underworld that kept them in the roots of the world tree.

50

Famous Vikings.

-Ragnar Lodbrock: feared warrior who carried out countless raids. He had 12 children, some of whom also stood out for their deeds. However, some historians believe that the character may be a legend and that the figure of several Nordic warriors is actually combined in this person.

-Lagertha: Ragnar's first wife and one of the most legendary Viking warriors. Still, some historians doubt her existence.

-Eric the Red: one of the best-known Vikings, a warrior who left his native Norway and reached Greenland.

-Freydis: Eric the Red's sister and one of the most famous Viking warriors.

-Leif Eriksson: son of Eric the Red and a prominent explorer like his father. He is believed to have been one of the first Europeans to reach North America.

-Harald Hardrada: Viking king who stood out for his bravery and military skills. He fought in several battles and became the last great Viking king.

-Olaf Tryggvason: another Viking king who ruled Norway in the 10th century. He converted to Christianity and tried to force his subjects to convert to Christianity as well.

-Thorfinn Karlsefni: Viking explorer who led an expedition to Vinland (North America) in the 11th century. He tried to establish a colony there, but ultimately failed.

-Egil Skallagrimsson: Viking poet and warrior who lived in Iceland in the 10th century. He is known for his literary skills and ferocity in battle.

-Ivar the Boneless: Viking warrior who fought in England in the 9th century. He is famous for leading the Great Heathen Army, which plundered and conquered much of England.

51

The Viking burial.

For many years, the Viking burial has been represented in this way: the deceased was placed in a small boat that was pushed out to sea or to the side.

An archer would shoot a burning arrow at the boat, which would burn as the family and friends watched the scene.

However, a few years ago, another reality about Viking burials came to light.

While the final burial usually involved a boat only in the case of the most important personalities, it was buried rather than burned.

In fact, in 2017, a tomb belonging to a female leader was discovered in the Viking city of Birka (Sweden), and in 2019, Norwegian archaeologists also found a boat grave that held two dead, the first burial having occurred almost 100 years before the second.

It is supposed that the second grave might have belonged to the granddaughter of the first.

Several rituals were performed during burials to prevent evil spirits from returning and spreading great harm.

They were particularly protected from the draugr, pestilent and terrifying creatures that arrived after death and contained a force capable of ravaging the world of the living.

52

Religious system.

The etymology of the days of the week in English comes from its deities:

Wednesday was dedicated to Odin, also known as Woden (Wednesday); Thursday to the famous hammer-wielding god Thor (Thursday); and Friday to the important goddess Freya (Friday).

The literal translation of Hávamál is "Sayings of the High One" or "Words of the High One".

It is one of the poems belonging to the Poetic Edda, a collection of poems written in Old Norse that are preserved in the medieval Icelandic manuscript known as Codex Regius.

53

What is the Codex Regius?

It is a handwritten document made in Iceland that contains several poems of pagan origin.

These poems were identified in 1643 by Brynjólfur Sveinsson as the poems contained in Snorri Sturluson's Prose Edda.

Sveinsson stated that the manuscript could have been authored by the Icelandic priest Saemundr Sigfússon, who compiled a series of poems whose origin he located in Viking Scandinavia (8th-13th centuries).

The poems collected in the Poetic Edda are believed to be of anonymous authorship or origin, as they were recited by troubadours and their transmission was also oral.

It is also said that later, several editors expanded the texts that made up the original Codex Regius with other poems and thus achieved the collection titled Poetic Edda.

54

The Poetic Edda is one of the main sources for learning about Norse mythology and Viking culture in general.

It is believed to have been written in Iceland in the 13th century, although some of the poems that make it up may be older.

The poems are anonymous and their authors are unknown.

The Poetic Edda is divided into two parts: the first is known as the Prose Edda or Snorri's Edda, and was written by the historian and poet Snorri Sturluson.

The second is the Lesser Edda, which includes the poems that are considered older and not related to Snorri's work.

The Poetic Edda presents a great number of gods and mythological creatures, such as Thor, Odin, Loki, Freya, among others.

The poems are full of adventures, feats, and battles, and one can see the importance that the Vikings gave to strength, courage, and honor.

The literary technique of kenning mentioned in the question is a prominent feature of skaldic poetry, a poetic style that developed in Viking culture and used complex images and metaphors to express ideas.

In the Poetic Edda, many examples of kenning can be found, making the reading more interesting and nuanced.

55

The Völuspá is considered one of the most important poems in the Poetic Edda.

It was written in Old Norse, and is believed to date back to the 10th century.

It is divided into 66 stanzas and tells the story of the origin of the world and its destruction, from the creation of the gods and human beings to Ragnarök, the final battle between the gods and the giants that will result in the destruction and rebirth of the world.

In the poem, a seeress (possibly the Viking goddess Völva) narrates the story to Odin, the king of the gods.

She describes the beginning of the world, the creation of the gods, the struggle between the gods and the giants, the birth of Loki and his role in the death of Balder, and the fate of the gods during Ragnarök.

The various creatures that inhabit the world, such as dwarves, giants, and valkyries, are also described.

The poem has a poetic and symbolic language, full of images and metaphors, and presents a dark and pessimistic portrayal of human and divine destiny.

Despite its antiquity, it remains an important source for understanding Viking religion and mythology, and has been the subject of many interpretations and studies.

Below is a small excerpt:

Then three giants appeared in the world, created by the great Architect; One was called Tiamat, the second was called Motsognir, and the third was named Ásgardhr.

Then the gods judged and the gods gathered; they gave form to beings and made worlds; the sun shone from the south on the stones of the mountains, and the fresh green of the grass sprouted from the newborn earth.

56

The Hávamál is a poem that is considered a kind of guide for the practical and moral life of the Vikings.

It is attributed to Odin, who imparts his wisdom in a series of maxims and advice for daily life.

The poem is divided into stanzas, each with two verses, and covers a wide range of topics, from personal ethics and morals to practical wisdom for daily life.

Among the main teachings of the Hávamál are the rules of hospitality, the importance of self-discipline, prudence and moderation in all things, as well as the value of wisdom and knowledge.

Additionally, the poem tells the story of how Odin discovered the runes, the magical alphabet of the Vikings, and how he used them to gain power and knowledge.

It also describes the use of spells and enchantments to protect oneself and others from malevolent forces.

Below is a small excerpt:

"It's best not to awaken someone who's sleeping; nor move from their place someone who's sitting; don't mock the fool or talk too much to him; it's good that no one knows your wisdom until you know it."

57

The poem "Vafþrúðnismál" tells the story of Odin, the main god of Norse mythology, who disguises himself as Gagnráðr and goes to the house of the giant Vafþrúðnir to test his wisdom and knowledge.

Odin and Vafþrúðnir begin a guessing game in which each asks questions and the other must answer correctly to win.

The questions and answers focus on Norse mythology and its characters.

In the poem, Odin shows his cunning and knowledge, and ultimately wins the competition by asking Vafþrúðnir a question he cannot answer.

The poem also describes Vafþrúðnir's house, which is said to be enormous and built of branches and roots of trees.

Additionally, several mythological animals are mentioned, such as the eagle that sits on top of the house and the wolf that guards the entrance.

In summary, "Vafþrúðnismál" is a poem from the Poetic Edda that narrates the guessing competition between Odin and the giant Vafþrúðnir, and provides valuable information about Norse mythology and its characters.

Below is a small excerpt:

"What was the name of the river that separates from Élivágar, and flows along the borders of the gods, before emptying into the sea?"

The river is called Slídr, which flows between frozen lands; it was the first river to exist, and the greatest ever seen.

58

**The poem Grímnismál is one of the poems
that make up the Poetic Edda.**

It is a poem in which Odin disguises himself as Grímnir and
tells the story of his torture at the hands of King Geirröd,
as well as his own nicknames.

The poem is largely a dialogue between Grímnir/Odin and
the young Agnar, who seems to have been sent by King
Geirröd to gather information about the strange visitor.

During the dialogue, Grímnir/Odin describes the world
of the gods and mythological beings, and reveals
some of the secrets of the universe.

The poem is important for its detailed description of the
structure of the universe according to Norse mythology,
as well as for the clues it offers about the
personality and character of Odin.

Here is a small excerpt:

"Nóatún, the hall of sailing, whose walls are of gold, and
the bright silver roof, which is in the world of the gods.
Hrist and Mist go from the horns of the called stags,
and Víðópnir too; the horns resound above Valhalla,
and announce to men their fate."

59

Skírnismál is a poem from the Poetic Edda that focuses on the story of the god Frey and his love for the beautiful giantess Gerd.

The poem begins with Skírnir, Frey's servant, asking the god about his melancholy.

Frey confesses that he fell in love with a beautiful woman he saw while sitting on Odin's throne, but he does not know how to find her.

Skírnir offers to go and find her and discovers that the woman is Gerd, daughter of the giant Hymir.

Skírnir sets out to help Frey win Gerd's heart, so he borrows Frey's magical horse and sword.

On behalf of Frey, Skírnir offers gifts to Gerd to win her heart, but she remains indifferent.

Skírnir becomes angry and threatens her with a spell if she does not accept Frey as her husband.

Finally, Gerd agrees to the proposal and agrees to marry Frey.

The poem is interesting because it shows the importance of magic and spells in Norse mythology, as well as the role of servants and messengers in the love relationships between gods and giants.

Additionally, it is one of the few poems in the Poetic Edda that focuses on the love story of a god, rather than on battles and violence.

Here is a small excerpt:

"Far on the plain of the gods I saw a shining house; Skirnir is the one who inhabits it, the most loyal of the Aesir. At the door I found the wolves tied up, the magnificent dog that roars I pushed aside to enter. From the highest seats the owner of the house greeted me; What do you want me to give you, so that you may address your lord?"

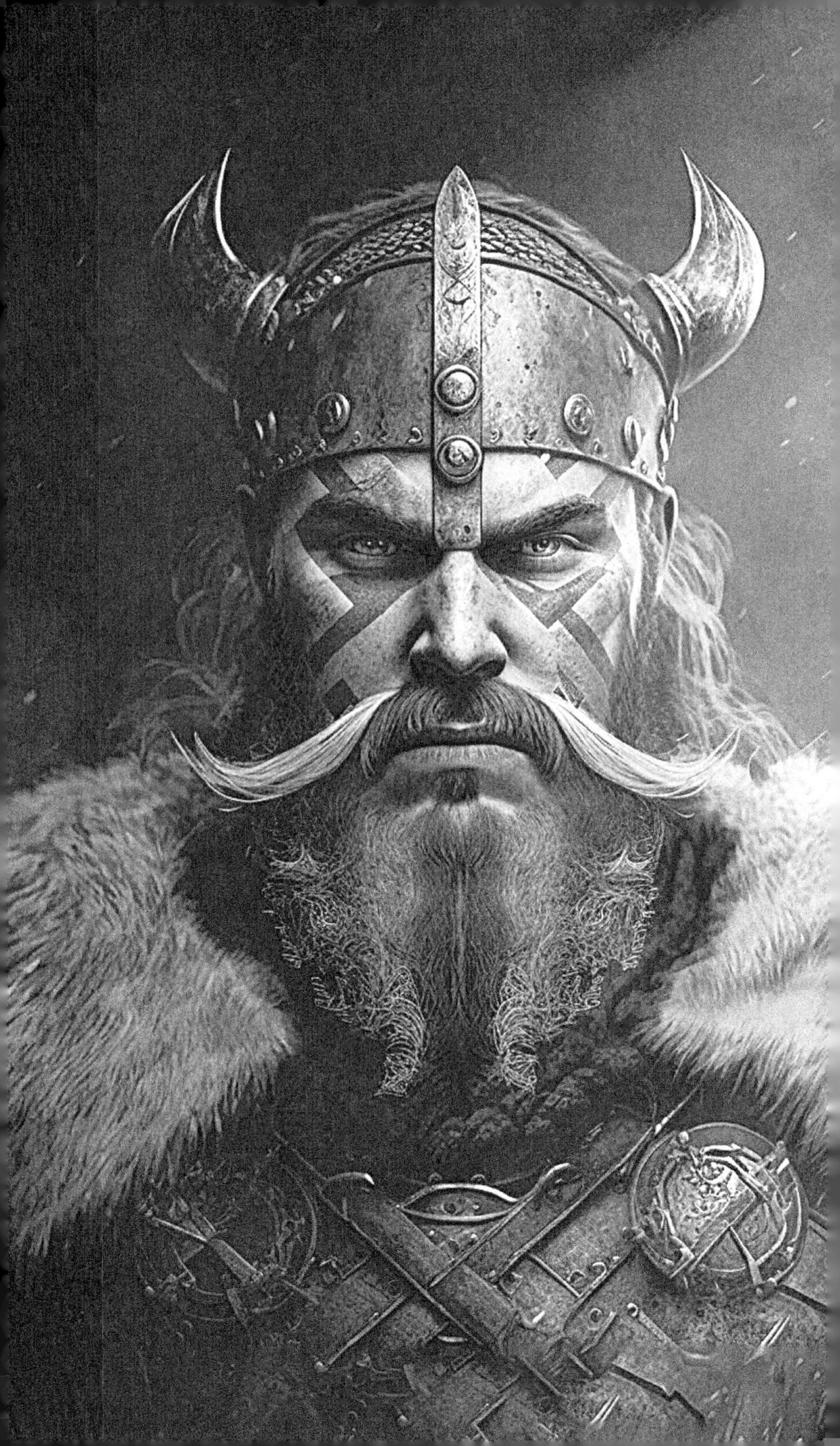

60

**The Poetic Edda is the Hárbarsljóð or
"The Poem of Hárbard".**

This poem tells the story of a boatman named Hárbard, who meets a man who turns out to be Thor in disguise.

The two begin to argue about who is more powerful and skilled, both in battle and in other abilities, such as magic and sexual prowess.

The discussion turns into a series of insults and mockery, and it is eventually revealed that Hárbard is actually the god Odin in disguise.

This suggests that Odin was testing Thor to see if he was strong and clever enough to be a true warrior and god.

Here's a small excerpt:

"Speak, Hárbard! Who are you who asks me? I am a wandering warrior seeking my way home. And who are you who challenges me? I am Hárbard, the wisest of boatmen. Wise, you say? We shall see, for I am Thor, the god of thunder, and none surpass my skills in battle."

61

The Poetic Edda of Hymiskviða.

It is also known as "The Song of Hymir".

This poem tells the story of Thor and his search for a giant cauldron that can hold enough mead to satisfy the thirst of all the gods.

To find the cauldron, Thor and his companion Týr travel to the realm of the giant Hymir, who possesses a large enough cauldron.

However, Hymir refuses to lend the cauldron unless Thor proves his strength by hunting a giant sea bull.

Thor finally accomplishes the feat, but the sea bull is so large that Thor and Hymir have difficulty dragging it back to the shore.

Eventually, Thor strikes the bull with his hammer Mjölnir and kills it, and they then bring it back to Hymir's house.

After that, Hymir agrees to lend his cauldron, and the gods celebrate a banquet in which they drink mead from it.

However, at the end of the poem, the sea giants rise up and threaten the gods, suggesting that the peace between the gods and giants is fragile and there is always the risk of it being broken.

62

The Poetic Edda of Lokasenna.

It is also known as "Loki's Sarcasm".

Lokasenna is a scene from a banquet at the home of the sea god Aegir, in which a series of insults and provocations erupt between Loki and the other Norse gods.

Loki begins to insult the gods one by one, exposing their flaws and weaknesses, and criticizing their behavior in various episodes of Norse mythology.

The gods, outraged by Loki's insults, challenge and threaten him, but Loki responds with even more provocations and sarcasm.

Finally, the poem culminates with the intervention of the god Heimdall, who chains Loki and throws him into a cave where he will be subjected to torture until the end of time.

Here's a small excerpt:

Loki began to insult the gods one by one, and thus he spoke of Bragi, the god of poetry: "Be quiet, Bragi, it never occurred to you to be brave in battle. You have never wielded a sword, never ridden a horse, nor fought against giants. Why do you call yourself Bragi?"

Bragi stood up, furious at the insult, and replied, "You're lying, Loki, and your words are malicious. I am the god of poetry, the one who inspires poets, and everyone who knows me knows that I am brave and honorable."

But Loki did not stop there, and continued to insult and provoke the gods at Aegir's feast, demonstrating his wickedness and his desire to create chaos and destruction in the world of the gods.

63

The Poetic Edda poem known as "Þrymskvöld" or "The Night of Þrymr" tells the myth of the theft of Thor's hammer, Mjolnir, by the giant Þrymr and the gods' quest to retrieve it.

The story begins with the theft of Mjolnir by the giant Þrymr, who demands it be given to him in exchange for the hand of the goddess Freyja in marriage.

The gods, desperate to recover the hammer, send Loki to Þrymr's house disguised as a woman in an attempt to deceive the giant and retrieve the hammer.

Þrymr, deceived by Loki, hands over the hammer and allows him to take it back to Asgard.

However, when the gods discover that the hammer is not real, they send Loki back to find out the truth.

Loki finally discovers that the real Mjolnir is in Þrymr's possession.

The gods then decide to disguise Thor as a bride and Loki as his companion and send them to Þrymr's house to retrieve the hammer.

When they arrive at the wedding ceremony, Þrymr places the hammer in "the bride's" possession as part of the dowry.

Thor takes the opportunity to retrieve his hammer and kill the giants.

The poem "Þrymskvöld" is an example of the stories told in Norse mythology and how gods and giants interact in their struggle for power.

64

Alvíssmál is a poem belonging to the Poetic Edda that tells the story of the conversation between Thor and the dwarf Alviss.

The dwarf arrives at Thor's house and asks for his daughter's hand in marriage, arguing that he has a right to her since he had helped forge Thor's hammer, Mjolnir.

Thor is not willing to grant him his daughter's hand and decides to test the dwarf's wisdom by asking him questions about the names of various objects and beings in the world.

The dwarf demonstrates a great knowledge of the world and answers all of Thor's questions.

However, the conversation lasts so long that dawn begins to break and the sun starts to rise.

The dwarf, who is a creature of the shadows, cannot bear the sunlight and begins to turn into stone, due to a curse that turns him to rock if exposed to daylight.

Despite Thor's pleas, Alviss eventually turns to stone.

The poem is interesting because it shows Thor's ability to test the wisdom of the beings that approach him, as well as the existence of a curse that affects dwarves who leave their caves and are exposed to daylight.

It also highlights Thor's sense of honor and justice, as he refuses to give his daughter in marriage to someone he does not believe is worthy of her.

65

Hávamál is a compilation of poems (25 precepts) that vary in tone and narrative form.

It is a great compendium of Scandinavian wisdom, which offers various pieces of advice about women, friends, conduct at banquets, hospitality towards guests, rules for traveling, and other matters, as well as adventures of Odin.

In other words, it could be considered a sort of Manual for the Good Viking or Odin's Tablets of the Law, as some verses are written from the perspective of the Nordic supreme god.

The content is both practical and metaphysical, and it has been translated into many languages with many different versions available.

66

Precepts of Hávamál

- The man who stands before a stranger's threshold should be cautious before stepping inside and carefully observe his path: who knows beforehand what enemies may be sitting there waiting for him in the hall?

- Hail to the host! A guest has arrived. Where should he sit? It is reckless to trust in one's luck before unfamiliar gates.

- Fire is needed by the newcomer, whose knees are numb with cold. Food and clean linen are needed by the man who has journeyed far.

- Water, too, that he may wash before eating, hand towel and a hearty welcome, good cheer and a respectful silence.

- He needs wit who travels far: it is easy to find oneself alone and lacking in judgement when seated among the foolish.

67

Precepts of Hávamál.

- A man should never boast of his wisdom, but hold it close and be sparing of speech when a wise guest arrives at his house: one's dearest friend is often the wisest.

- A guest should be cautious who comes to the banquet and sit quiet and attentive, with ears open and eyes alert: so he protects himself, the wise man.

- Happy is the man who enjoys in his lifetime the esteem and praise of all; ill counsel is often given by those of wicked heart.

- Happy is the man who in his life finds praise and joy; often evil counsel has been given by a man of wicked heart.

- No better burden can a man carry on the road than plenty of wisdom: it is the best provision for journeys through the unknown, and no matter how great the hardship, it will never fail him.

68

Havamal precepts.

-There's no better burden for the journey than great wisdom; excessive thirst for liquor is the worst provision for the roads.

-The so-called good beer is not as good as it's said to be, for the more a man drinks, the more he loses his judgement.

-The bird of oblivion, hovering over banquets, is called the heron; it steals men's judgement. I was imprisoned in the feathers of that bird in Gunnlod's estate.

-I was drunk, I was drunk in Fjalar's hall; it was well drunk if the man's judgement returns after the feast.

-The son of a king is silent and thoughtful, bold in war; let every man be content and joyful until the day he dies.

69

Havamal precepts.

- The fool hopes to live forever if he avoids quarrels, but old age gives him little respite if spears should be thrust at him.

- The fool opens wide his eyes when he comes as a guest, mumbles or says nothing; but as soon as he gets a drink, he is very talkative.

- Only he knows who has traveled far and wide; everyone governs himself with judgement, and he has a keen mind.

- Do not cling to the horn, drink mead with caution, speak if necessary, or be silent; no one will accuse you of stupidity if you go to bed early.

- The glutton who cannot use his judgement eats and ruins his life; the belly of the senseless man is a source of mockery among prudent people.

70

Havamal precepts.

-Cattle know when to go home and leave the pastures; but the fool has no notion of how much his belly can hold.

-The mean and wicked man laughs at anything; but he doesn't know, and should know, that he too has faults.

-An ignorant man spends his nights awake, thinking about anything; thus, he is exhausted when morning comes, and his misery remains the same.

-An ignorant man thinks that those who laugh with him are his friends; but he doesn't know that they speak ill of him when he sits among the wise.

-An ignorant man thinks that everyone who laughs with him is his friend; but when he has a lawsuit, he sees that few speak for him.

71

Viking proverbs about friendship.

-A man honors his friend with affection, responds to a gift with a gift. He responds to laughter with laughter, and to trickery with deceit.

-If you manage to find a loyal friend and want him to be useful to you, open your heart to him, send him gifts, and travel often to see him.

-A man without friends is like a bare birch, without leaves or bark, lonely on a barren hill.

-Be a friend to your friends. Respond to a gift with another gift, to a smile with another smile, and to a lie as if you hadn't heard it.

-A guest should leave on time and not overstay their welcome; even a friend becomes annoying if they stay too long.

-It's hard to visit a bad friend even if it's on the way. But it's pleasant to visit a good friend even if their house is far away.

-I never met anyone so rich and noble who didn't like to receive gifts, nor so generous that they didn't want to receive anything in return.

72

Viking proverbs about intelligence.

-There is no better luggage to carry than sanity and a clear mind. In foreign lands, it's more useful than gold and helps the poor out of trouble.

-Whoever always speaks and never keeps silent says many foolish things. A loose tongue causes problems and often belittles a man.

-The best load a man can carry is too much common sense; the worst, too much drink.

-Beer isn't as good as they say. The more you drink, the less you reason and lose your own judgment.

-The wretched and ill-born man makes jokes and mocks everything. He doesn't realize something more obvious: his own flaws.

-Truly wise is the traveler who moves around the world. He can sense the prevailing mood by being sensible and sane.

-The sensible man will flee the room if a guest insults another. Ridicule and mockery often annoy if there are hostile men at the table.

73

Viking sayings about power and wealth.

- If you eat cherries with the powerful, you risk the pits raining down on your nose.

- Who knows how many enemies you have around the table!

- Close to the king, close to the scaffold.

- Neither poverty forces anyone to steal nor wealth prevents it.

- Misfortune also visits the rich, but it visits the poor twice.

- In an agreement, beware that one party doesn't end up with the sword and the other with the sheath.

- Two can lie until a third one hangs.

- Ambition and revenge are always hungry.

74

Viking phrases about enjoying life.

-Live with enthusiasm while you're alive, the agile always comes out ahead. I saw the flames of a mansion, but at the door lay a dead man.

-The best thing about life is life itself. Make sure you enjoy every moment and leave a good name behind. There is nothing better than being alive and happy.

-A coward thinks he will live forever if he avoids his enemies; but no man escapes old age, even if he survives the spears.

-A man of respect should be reserved, thoughtful, and brave in battle. All men should maintain good humor until the end comes.

-A lame man can still ride a horse, a man without hands can still shepherd sheep, and a deaf man can still kill; it is better to be blind than to burn on the funeral pyre. It is the dead who can do nothing.

-Better a free bird than a captive king.

-You should enjoy your gains while you remain in this world. What you leave for your friend may end up in the hands of your enemy. Who knows what might happen...

-It is good to rise early if you want to go and fight and take others' lives and goods. The wolf lying down does not fill its mouth. No one triumphs while lying down.

-Fire is healthy for all beings, just like the rays of the sun. Blessed is he who maintains his health and knows how to live without vices.

-Fortune dies, family dies, oneself also dies. But there is something that will always remain: the good reputation of the deceased.

75

Viking proverbs about prudence.

-Before entering a place, look where you can get out.

-Do not praise the day until it is evening; do not praise a woman until her funeral pyre; do not praise a sword until you have tried it; do not praise a maiden until she is married; do not praise the ice until you have crossed it; do not praise the beer until you have drunk it.

-Do not stray an inch from your weapons outside of your home.

-Crumbs are also bread.

-The house of one who mocks will end up burning.

-In making an agreement, be careful that one party does not end up with the sword and the other with the sheath.

-When passing through another's door, look to the right, look to the left.

-The mouth rules the land, but the hand rules the sea.

-The sensible man does not presume to be wise. He walks with caution and tact. He goes to the village quietly, avoiding entanglements. His most faithful ally never fails him: His prudence that accompanies him.

76

Thor.

Son of Odin, the god of gods, Thor represents strength, power, and war.

Blonde or red-haired beard and fierce gaze were part of the physical characteristics with which he was often described, although almost as important as him was his weapon.

Thor is always depicted wielding a hammer known as Mjolnir, forged by dwarves.

His means of transportation was an imposing chariot that was pulled by goats whose footsteps were marked by sounds that emulated lightning and thunder.

77

Odin.

He was the god of gods, to whom homage had to be paid.

Father of Thor, he possessed some of the characteristics that he passed on to his son: strength, skill, war, intelligence, and cunning.

His raison d'être was knowledge and wisdom.

He transformed himself to acquire more intellect, and he was always accompanied by ravens.

In order to carry out an increase in intelligence, Odin was associated with human and animal sacrifices, which earned him the loss of an eye.

78

Frigg.

She is the wife of Odin
and stepmother of Thor.

This Viking deity represented love,
fertility, marriage, motherhood,
and the art of the home.

Her special power was the ability to
prophesy, know and understand the
fate of all humans, as well as being
the only one, after Odin, to be able
to occupy the throne of the gods
and observe the universe.

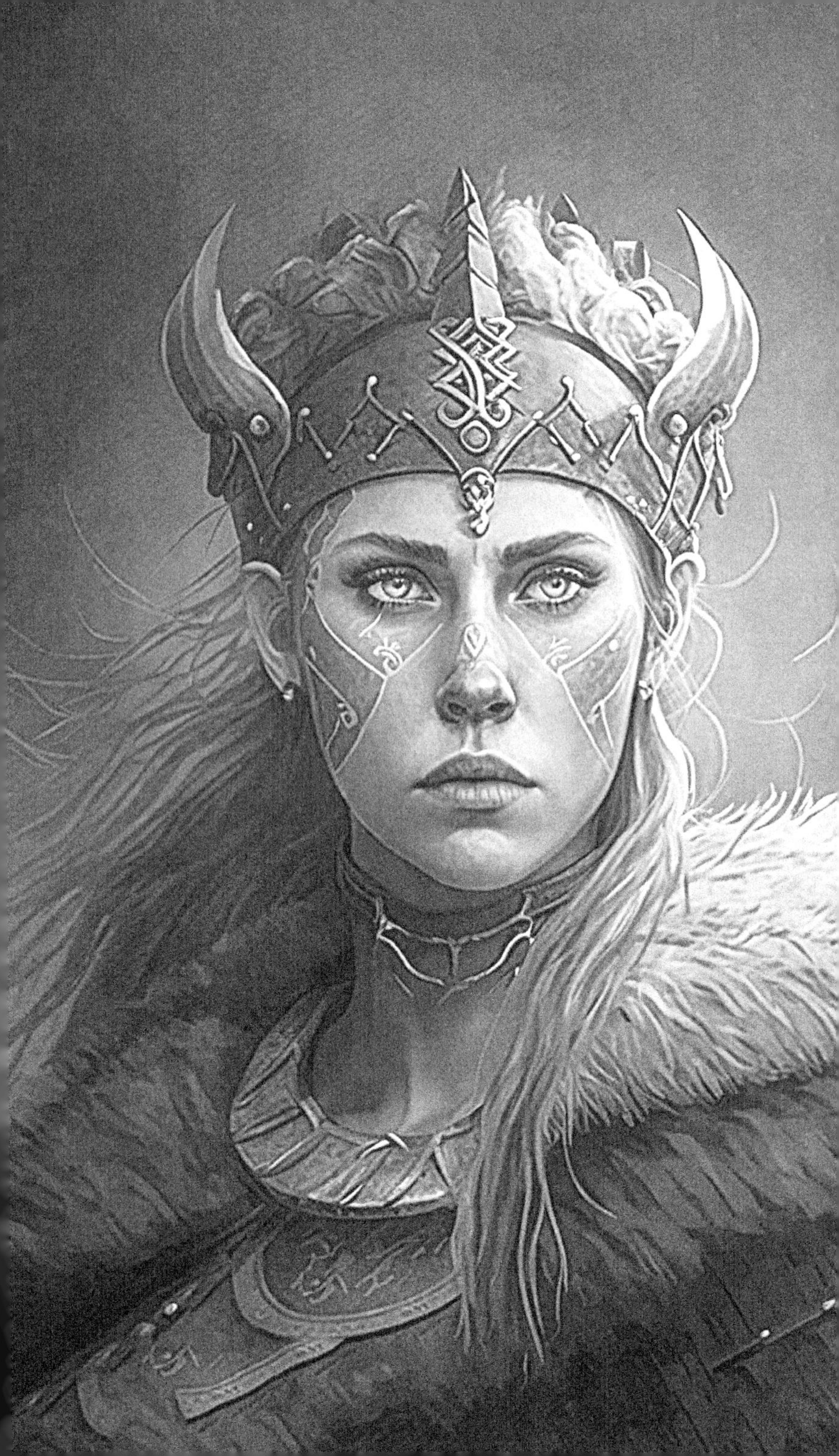

79

Tyr.

The god Tyr is considered the ultimate warrior among all Viking gods.

Although most of his encounters, stories, and narratives are related to war and strength, he was not an exclusively brutish character, but also had iconographies associated with wisdom and laws.

Similarly, he also made a sacrifice of his own and had his left arm amputated so that the gods could save the world from the wolf Fenrir.

It is worth noting that only Thor surpassed him in terms of physical strength.

80

Freyja.

She was the goddess of love and fertility, beauty and romance.

She was madly in love with her husband Odr.

It is said that when he was away from her, Freyja would cry and, because of how beautiful she was, tears of gold would fall from her eyelashes.

For these reasons, among others, she was one of the most respected deities, although from a modern perspective she seems more like a collection of characteristics traditionally associated with femininity.

Her clothing was worthy of what she represented.

Beautiful, shiny necklaces and precious, hypnotic plumage that allowed her to fly between underworlds, and a carriage pulled by wonderful felines were among the objects with which she was represented.

Although she was the least warlike deity, she accompanied soldiers and gods to war to instill security and motivation, as she was considered wise.

81

Loki.

According to Norse mythology, Loki is the son of the giants Laufey and Farbauti, and is characterized by his ability to deceive and sow chaos.

In fact, technically he is not a god, but a mysterious entity that mixes with the gods or even impersonates one.

There is very little information about Loki and it is not clear to what extent he was part of the original pantheon of Norse mythology; however, his influence has been reflected in Western culture through all kinds of stories, as well as operas, movies, novels,...

82

Yggdrasil: the sacred tree.

The beliefs of the Nordic peoples related to cosmology aim to explain not only the origin but also the evolution of the universe and the laws that order the functioning of the physical world.

The 9 worlds are distributed in the sacred ash tree Yggdrasil, which serves as a support for the universe; and in whose branches the hawk Veðrfölnir has its home, sitting between the eyes of an unnamed eagle along with a squirrel named Ratatösk, a dragon named Níðhöggr, and four stags, Dáinn, Dvalinn, Duneyrr, and Duraþrór, who eat the tree's buds.

Near its roots dwell the norns.

Yggdrasil has three roots that lead to the worlds of Asgard, Jötunheim, and Niflheim, and are nourished by their respective springs.

The root that reaches Niflheim is mercilessly attacked by Nidhogg, the winged dragon, which gradually eats its wood, as well as by four venomous vipers that contaminate the water that sustains it.

The wounds of Yggdrasil are healed by the goddess Urd in Asgard, lovingly applying a special balm.

The head of the god Mimir is located in the spring that leads to Jotunheim, and is frequently consulted by Odin, as it is an oracle that knows the past, present, and future of everything.

On the other hand, along the longitudinal extension of the sacred trunk of Yggdrasil runs a squirrel that constantly transports the insults that Nidhogg tells the eagle and vice versa.

83

Origin of the nine worlds.

At first, there was a deep darkness from which two worlds emerged, the world of fire and the world of ice, which expanded slowly and upon contact generated a minor cataclysm in the cosmos.

From this cataclysm, blocks of frost and a thick mist emerged, as part of the world of ice liquefied; and from this water, Ymir was born, considered the father of the ice giants, who was nursed by the cow Audumla.

The giant Ymir fell asleep after having been satisfied and began to sweat, then a woman and a man of his kind emerged from the giant's left arm, and became the propagators of the lineage of the ice giants.

Simultaneously, Audumla licked the salty frost rocks and uncovered a silhouette of a human being, known as Buri and identified as the ancestor of the deities.

Buri, in turn, had a son whom he named Bor, who was the father of Odin, Vili, whose meaning is "will," and Ve, which means priest, gods who fought against the ice giants and, by killing Ymir, defeated them.

The gods took the corpse of Ymir and created the sky with the concave part of the skull, the seas and lakes with his blood, and the earth with his flesh, and at the end of their creative work, the universe was formed with nine worlds.

84

Niflheim.

It is one of the nine worlds in Norse mythology, located in the far north of the cosmos.

This world is associated with cold, darkness, fog, and ice, and is considered the world of the dead.

It is said that Niflheim is a lonely world, populated by ice giants and other beings related to cold and snow.

In the center of Niflheim lies a great spring called Hvergelmir, from which the twelve rivers of Niflheim flow.

Among them is the famous Midgard serpent, which encircles the world of the living.

In addition, it is believed that Helheim, the abode of the goddess Hel, is located in Niflheim, where the spirits of the dead who are not brave or honorable go.

Helheim is described as a somber and cold place, where the souls of the dead live in a kind of eternal mist, without any hope of escape.

85

Muspellheim.

It is one of the nine worlds in Norse mythology, located in the south of the Norse cosmology.

It is the world of fire and extreme heat, in contrast to the world of eternal ice, Niflheim.

According to mythology, Muspellheim is the home of fire giants, as well as the lord of fires, Surtr, who guards the entrance to the world with his flaming sword.

In addition, it is believed that the flames that will unleash Ragnarok, the end of the Norse world, will come from this world.

Muspellheim is described as a place of immense brightness and scorching heat, so intense that even the gods cannot endure it.

However, some gods and divine beings are immune to fire, such as Surtur, who is able to control fire and flame at will.

It is believed that Muspellheim and Niflheim joined together at the beginning of time to create the giant Ymir, from whose body the world was formed.

86

Asgard is considered the home of the Aesir gods, and is described as a walled and fortified city located at the center of the universe.

Access to Asgard is protected by the god Heimdall, who watches over the Bifrost Bridge, which is the only entrance to the city.

Within the walls of Asgard are several halls and buildings, each of which has its own function and is dedicated to a particular god.

One of the most important halls is Valhalla, the hall of the warriors who died in combat.

The warrior gods, led by Odin, are responsible for selecting the best warriors who have died in battle and taking them to Valhalla, where they spend eternity fighting and feasting with the gods.

Another important building in Asgard is Odin's palace, known as Gladsheim.

This palace is the center of political and religious activity for the gods, and is where the assemblies of the Aesir gods are held.

Thor's castle, Bliskirnir, which is made of gold and is the home of the god of thunder and his goats, is also located in Asgard.

In addition, Asgard is home to the palace of the goddesses, Vingolf, which is the meeting place for the goddesses of Norse mythology.

In this place, the goddesses dedicate themselves to weaving and conversing.

87

Midgard, known as "Middle Earth", is a spherical world surrounded by a great ocean that is encircled by the body of a monstrous serpent, which prevents the ocean from overflowing.

It is a world created to be inhabited by humans, but in which dwarves also coexist.

The first pair of human beings, a man and a woman, were created by the gods Odin, Ve, and Vili, from two logs found on a beach.

Meanwhile, the dwarves, who were worms in the corpse of Ymir, emerged in Middle Earth and the gods gave them human form and reason.

88

Jötunheim.

It is actually the home of the giants, not their prison.

The prison of the giants is called Útgarðr.

Jötunheim is one of the nine worlds of Norse mythology, and it is the home of the giants, also known as jötnar.

These beings are considered enemies of the gods, and they are often involved in conflicts with them.

In Jötunheim, there are various mountains, rivers, and forests, and its inhabitants are described as beings of great stature and strength.

Some of the most well-known giants of Norse mythology include Thrym, who stole Thor's hammer, and Utgarda-Loki, who challenged Thor to a strength duel.

Despite being considered enemies of the gods, marriages between them have occasionally been recorded.

For example, the goddess Skadi married the giant Thiazi and lived in Jötunheim for a time.

89

Vanaheim.

In this world live the Vanir, who are the gods of prosperity and fertility, and they are subject to the Aesir.

Snorri introduces Vanaheim in this way:

"Thus it is known that a great sea enters into Nörvasund (Strait of Gibraltar to the land of Jerusalem). From this sea another great sea-like inlet stretches to the northeast, and is called the Black Sea, and it divides the three parts of the earth; of which the eastern part is called Asia, and the western part is called by some Europe, by others Enea. Northward from the Black Sea extends Svíþjóð the Great, or the Cold. On the south side of the mountains which stretch beyond the inhabited lands, a river runs through Svíþjóð, the correct name of which is Tanais (present-day Don River, Russia), but it was formerly called Tanakvísl, or Vanakvísl, and it empties into the Black Sea. The country of the people of Vanakvísl was called Vanaland, or Vanaheimr; and the river separates the three parts of the world, where the eastern part is called Asia, and the western part Europe."

90

Alfheim.

It is believed that this world is located at the top of the cosmic tree Yggdrasil, very close to Asgard, the home of the gods.

Most descriptions of Alfheim speak of a beautiful and bright place, full of trees and flowers.

In this world, the light elves live in small villages and cities, and dedicate themselves to craftsmanship, music, and poetry.

The ljósálfar (light elves) are believed to be kind and benevolent creatures who enjoy helping mortals in times of need.

In Norse stories, light elves are often described as beautiful and ethereal beings who possess great wisdom and knowledge of the universe.

On the other hand, the svartálfar (dark elves) are considered a kind of sub-race of elves who inhabit the mountains and caves.

Unlike the light elves, it is said that dark elves are more somber and mysterious beings, who are often associated with black magic and darkness.

In some stories, it is said that dark elves are enemies of the gods and mortals, and that they try to influence the human world for their own purposes.

91

Svartalfheim.

It is the underworld, the dwelling place of the dark elves.

The dark elves are creatures with characteristics similar to dwarves (duergar) and are the counterpart of the light elves, the Ljósálfar.

The original Svartalfar worked the forges on the lowest level of the world tree.

Their role and appearance vary throughout folklore, but they are sometimes mentioned with dark or black skin as a result of their work in the forge.

The Dökkálfar ("Dark Elves") are ancestral guardians who protect people, although they can also be threatening, especially when treated rudely.

They usually try to avoid light, although they are not necessarily underground.

92

Helheim.

It is located beneath Midgard and is the place where those who die but are not worthy of the privilege of accompanying the gods in Asgard go, either because they died of old age or some illness.

In the center of Helheim is the island of Aastrand, where a torture chamber is located to subject those who acted vilely throughout their lives.

And next to this, the construction process of the Naiafarer Nalfgar takes place with the nails of the dead, which is the drakkar that the bands of evil will use to attack Asgard on the day of Ragnarök, and it will be the end of the known world.

93

What were the dwarves like in Norse mythology?

Most of the time, they were described as beings who lived underground and were known for being great blacksmiths and inventors.

For example, when Loki needed to acquire golden hair for Sif, he visited two groups of characters that are often interpreted as dwarves.

Not only did they create a new head of hair for Sif, but they also invented other magical creations as gifts for the gods.

These hardworking and cunning dwarves fit well into the modern image of the race, but the definition of a dwarf in Norse mythology sometimes seems more ambiguous.

For example, a group of dwarves mentioned in the same story are the sons of Ivaldi, who in another part are called the father of Idunn. Idunn, the goddess of youth, is often called an elf instead of a dwarf.

Many dwarves in the tales are villainous characters.

Kvasir, for example, was killed by two dwarves who mixed his blood into the Mead of Poetry after he was invited to their home.

In another legend, a dwarf named Alviss wants to marry Thor's daughter.

The god keeps him in conversation until the sun comes up, at which point Alviss turns to stone.

The idea that dwarves cannot be in sunlight is not mentioned anywhere else, and many named dwarves live on the surface.

The character of Alviss seems to have more in common with the typical representation of a troll than a dwarf.

While their strength is sometimes highlighted, their height rarely is.

In fact, the names of some dwarves suggest that they are exceptionally tall and no shorter than the average human.

Fullangr, for example, means "sufficiently tall," while Har translates as "tall."

94

Norse mythology: Trolls.

They are described as huge and hairy beings,
very strong but very slow.

Trolls live in caves or isolated mountains, living together
in small family units and rarely helping humans.

Troll is a term applied to Jötnar and is mentioned
throughout the Old Norse corpus.

The skald Bragi Boddason tells a tale in which he had
a conversation with an unnamed Troll woman.

Numerous stories are recorded about Trolls, in which they are
described as extremely old and occasionally as man-eaters
who turn to stone upon contact with sunlight.

The absence of Trolls and Jötnar in the regions of Scandinavia
is explained by Thor's effectiveness in fighting these beings.

Church bells were rung to scare away Trolls,
emulating the thunderclaps of the sky.

In Beowulf, the monster Grendel is compared
and represented as a Troll.

In Denmark, there is a subspecies of Troll smaller
than the size of a human known as Troll-Folk.

95

How many women did the Vikings have?

Men could have several women under their roof and these relationships were officially allowed.

Most of them were slaves, although there could be free women in the harem.

In the event that the Viking officially married two women, all the children were considered legitimate.

However, it should be noted that most marriages were monogamous and polygamy was only allowed in certain situations, such as when the first wife could not have children.

In addition, most women living under a Viking man's roof were wives or concubines, not slaves.

Women had an important role in Viking society, and some of them had a high social status, such as goðar-konas, women who wielded political and religious power in their community.

Regarding the legitimacy of children, all children of a Viking man were considered legitimate, regardless of whether their father was married to their mother or not.

However, the children of a legitimate wife had a higher social status than those of a concubine or slave.

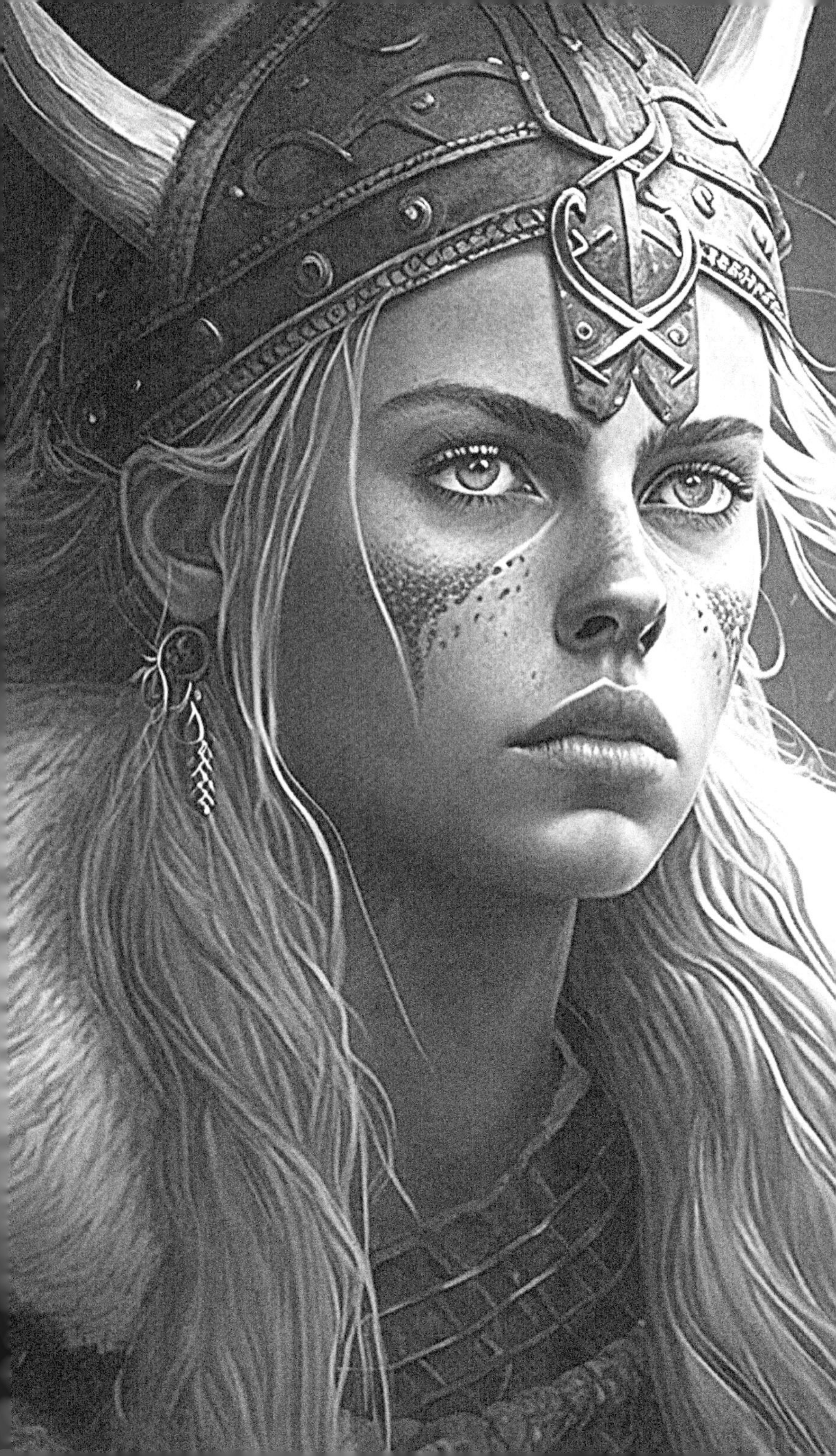

96

Skjaldmö: the shieldmaidens.

Regarding historical records, there are not many that mention female warriors, but they exist.

Lagertha appears to be a historical figure, as she is mentioned by Saxo Grammaticus in his famous work Gesta Danorum.

The historian mentions her as the first wife of Ragnar Lodbrok, whom she met during a battle.

Saxo recounts that it was the shieldmaiden's ferocity in battle that enamored Ragnar.

Later, he writes that despite divorcing her, Lagertha lent Ragnar 120 ships for a battle.

The last mention of Lagertha is that she killed her second husband to take his place as Jarl.

Another possible proof of the existence of female warriors in northern Scandinavia can be found in Birka.

A grave has been discovered there in which a skeleton was buried with weapons and other warrior ornaments.

Recent DNA studies indicate that the skeleton belongs to a woman, which leads to the conclusion that it could be a female warrior or skjaldmö.

97

Sexual slavery.

Viking culture was always characterized by the use of slavery in their sexual practices.

Especially as the warriors conquered and plundered distant lands, such as around the Volga basin, the trade of slaves became a very prosperous business.

In this way, they brought women to their villages for their personal parties.

98

Lesbianism.

Viking women were allowed to do anything if they fulfilled their important reproductive function.

For example, if they raised strong children, then their lesbian relationships were allowed.

In that case, the man could not be accused of being unmanly.

Interestingly, in Viking culture, free women also enjoyed the same sexual freedom as men.

Homosexuality.

Homosexuality was not well regarded in Viking society, but it was not a taboo or sacrilege.

In the community, sexual relationships between men were normal, but only if they were active.

If they were passive, society repudiated and mocked them.

The curious thing is that homosexual preferences mattered very little, as long as the man married, had children, and followed the imposed social norms.

99

Death penalty for abusers.

Women were protected against sexual assaults.

If abuse was proven, the accused was sentenced to death.

The violation of a free woman was one of the worst offenses against coexistence.

However, it is important to note that in many cases, justice in the Viking age was carried out locally and there was no unified judicial system.

This means that punishments and laws could vary from one place to another and be influenced by cultural and religious factors.

100

Sex with young women.

In Viking villages, according to historian James H. Barrett, selective infanticide of girls generated an excess of young men.

Because of this, Viking warriors had to compete for them and that is why they sailed to other lands in search of wealth to have more possibilities in marriage.

Viking women married at a very young age to older men who had to have a lot of land and economic power.

This practice was also common in the Middle Ages worldwide.

Fertility and procreation were always very important elements in their culture.

101

Ragnarok.

It is an apocalyptic event that appears in Norse mythology and in Viking cosmology.

It is considered as the end of the world and the end of gods and men.

The word "Ragnarok" is composed of two terms: "Ragna" which means "of the gods" and "Rok" which means "destiny".

Thus, the term translates as "the destiny of the gods".

According to Norse mythology, Ragnarok will be a catastrophic event in which gods, giants, and men will face each other in an epic battle that will end with the destruction of the world and the death of many of the main characters of Norse mythology.

Among the most relevant details of Ragnarok, the following are found:

-According to the prophecy, Ragnarok will be unleashed when the eternal winter covers the earth and the sun darkens.

-The gods and the giants will fight in a battle that will take place in the plains of Vigrid. Odin, the king of the gods, and the fire giant Surt will lead their respective forces.

-Thor, the god of thunder, will fight against the serpent Jormungand, his archenemy, in a battle that will end with the death of both.

-Freyr, the god of fertility, will die at the hands of the giant Surtr.

-The wolf Fenrir, son of Loki, will be released from his chains and will face Odin, killing him in the final battle.

If you have enjoyed the information and anecdotes presented in this book, we would like to ask you to leave a review on Amazon.

Your opinion is extremely valuable to us and to other readers who are looking for accurate and entertaining information about the Vikings.

Furthermore, your review will help us improve our work and continue creating high-quality content for history enthusiasts.

We understand that leaving a review can be a cumbersome process, but we would love for you to take a few minutes of your time to share your thoughts and opinions with us.

Your support is very important to us and it helps us continue creating content that is of interest to Viking culture enthusiasts.

Thank you for your support.

May Odin guide your path and protect you from any danger!

★ ★ ★ ★ ★

Printed in Great Britain
by Amazon